BLUE BANNER BIOGRAPHY

Russell WILSON

Cliff Mills

Mitchell Lane
PUBLISHERS
P.O. Box 196
Hockessin, Delaware 19707
Visit us on the web: www.mitchelllane.com

Printing   1   2   3   4   5   6   7   8   9

Blue Banner Biographies

5 Seconds of Summer	Ice Cube	Miguel Tejada
Abby Wambach	Ja Rule	Mike Trout
Adele	Jamie Foxx	Nancy Pelosi
Alicia Keys	Jason Derulo	Natasha Bedingfield
Allen Iverson	Jay-Z	Nicki Minaj
Ashanti	Jennifer Hudson	One Direction
Ashlee Simpson	Jennifer Lopez	Orianthi
Ashton Kutcher	Jessica Simpson	Orlando Bloom
Avril Lavigne	JJ Watt	P. Diddy
Blake Lively	J. K. Rowling	Peyton Manning
Blake Shelton	Joe Flacco	Pharrell Williams
Bow Wow	John Legend	Pink
Brett Favre	Justin Berfield	Pit Bull
Britney Spears	Justin Timberlake	Prince William
Bruno Mars	Kanye West	Queen Latifah
CC Sabathia	Kate Hudson	Rihanna
Carrie Underwood	Katy Perry	Robert Downey Jr.
Chris Brown	Keith Urban	Robert Pattinson
Chris Daughtry	Kelly Clarkson	Ron Howard
Christina Aguilera	Kenny Chesney	Russell Wilson
Ciara	Ke$ha	Sean Kingston
Clay Aiken	Kevin Durant	Selena
Cole Hamels	Kristen Stewart	Shakira
Condoleezza Rice	Lady Gaga	Shia LaBeouf
Corbin Bleu	Lance Armstrong	Shontelle Layne
Daniel Radcliffe	Leona Lewis	Soulja Boy Tell 'Em
David Ortiz	Lil Wayne	Stephenie Meyer
David Wright	Lionel Messi	Taylor Swift
Derek Jeter	Lindsay Lohan	T.I.
Drew Brees	LL Cool J	Timbaland
Dwyane Wade	Ludacris	Tim McGraw
Eminem	Luke Bryan	Tim Tebow
Eve	Mariah Carey	Toby Keith
Fergie	Mario	Usher
Flo Rida	Mary J. Blige	Vanessa Anne Hudgens
Gwen Stefani	Mary-Kate and Ashley Olsen	Will.i.am
Hope Solo	Megan Fox	Zac Efron

Library of Congress Cataloging-in-Publication Data
Mills, Cliff, 1947–
  Russell Wilson / by Cliff Mills.
     pages cm. — (Blue Banner Biographies)
  Includes bibliographical references and index.
  Audience: Age: 5-9.
  Audience: Grade 1 to Grade 4.
  ISBN 978-1-68020-083-6 (library bound)
  1. Wilson, Russell, 1988– Juvenile literature. 2. Football players—United States—Biography— Juvenile literature. 3. Quarterbacks (Football)—United States--Biography—Juvenile literature. I. Title.
  GV939.W545M55 2015
  796.332092 — dc23
                                                                               2015003207
eBook ISBN: 978-1-68020-084-3

ABOUT THE AUTHOR: Clifford Mills has written many biographies about world leaders and sports superstars. He is a Carter-Woodson Award Honorable Mention from the National Council for Social Studies. Like Russell Wilson's father, he played baseball for Dartmouth College, but he never could have been a wide receiver for the San Diego Chargers. Mills lives in Jacksonville, Florida with his wife Rosemary, his baseball trophies, and Super Bowl XLVIII memories.

In the middle of a confetti storm, Wilson raises the Lombardi Trophy high over his head to celebrate the Seattle Seahawks' victory over the Denver Broncos in Super Bowl XLVIII at MetLife Stadium on February 2, 2014.

They Are the Champions

*E*very year, the Super Bowl is America's biggest football game. It got even bigger when it was held at MetLife Stadium in Rutherford, New Jersey, on February 2, 2014. With over 111 million television viewers tuning in, Super Bowl XLVIII was watched by more people than any event in American history.

Fans started filing into the stadium in the early afternoon, some wearing Seahawk blues and greens, some wearing Bronco orange. The pre-game tension built, amplified by marching bands, performers from Broadway musicals, and fireworks. On the last note of the National Anthem, nine US Army helicopters flew over the stadium in a U-formation. The game began with a roar.

That game should have been an epic struggle. The National Football League's (NFL) best offense, the Denver Broncos, was playing the best defense, the Seattle Seahawks. The Broncos were led by future Hall-of-Fame quarterback Peyton Manning. Some argue that he is the best quarterback ever. A second-year player named Russell Wilson quarterbacked the Seahawks. Many experts, who said he was too short to play professional football, had doubted him. Some said this Super Bowl would be Manning's chance to show again that he was truly the league's most valuable player (MVP).

Manning had a disastrous start. The snap from center on the first play flew over his head. It was a sign of things to come. Soon it was Wilson, not Manning, who was throwing perfect passes to several different receivers. Some passes were laser-straight. Some floated softly, landing in between defenders.

On one play in the first quarter, Wilson took the snap from center near mid-field. He looked down the field to see who was coming open. He then launched a long pass that hung in the air long enough for Seahawk wide receiver Doug Baldwin to run under it. It was just over the head of the Bronco defender. Fox Sports broadcaster Joe Buck shouted, "What a throw!"

Some professional football players can run very fast, some can throw a football very hard, and some can throw a football with great accuracy. Very few can do all three at the same time. Russell Wilson can and did. He was a magic man, dazzling the crowd and breaking the Broncos.

Wilson went on to throw two touchdowns in the biggest game of his life. He had no interceptions and no mistakes. William Rhoden of *The New York Times* wrote that Wilson was "the Seahawks dream-maker . . . He did everything an MVP should do." Seattle won Super Bowl XLVIII, 43 to 8.

After the game, Wilson held the Lombardi Trophy high over his head. A blizzard of green, blue, and white confetti surrounded him. He and his team were world champions.

He told reporters, "At the beginning of the season, I told our guys, 'Hey, why not us?' We wanted to win it all." His father had always encouraged him to go after his dreams.

A few days later, hundreds of thousands of people in Seattle lined its downtown streets to honor their heroes.

Children were let out of school. The fans had prided themselves on being the "12th man," (Seahawks loud, sold out crowds became known as the 12th man) yelling so loudly at games that they set a world record for noise. Under a brilliant cold and blue winter sky, chants of WIL-SON, WIL-SON could be heard mixing with SEA-HAWKS, SEA-HAWKS. Wilson had captured their hearts.

In May 2014, most of the team visited the White House. President Barack Obama celebrated the Seattle defense, nicknamed the "Legion of Boom." But then he talked about Russell Wilson, telling reporters, "He's only the second African-American quarterback to ever win the Super Bowl . . . Part of the reason Russell inspired a lot of folks is he's been proving the doubters wrong for a very long time. For years, folks said he's too short to succeed as quarterback in the NFL."

Russell Wilson, his team, and their fans had made history. Wilson's own personal history began many miles from Seattle.

> *Russell Wilson, his team, and their fans had made history. Wilson's own personal history began many miles from Seattle.*

When Wilson quarterbacked the North Carolina State University Wolfpack, he was a strong-armed leader who inspired teammates and fans alike.

A Gifted and Talented Family

*R*ussell Carrington Wilson was born on November 29, 1988, in Cincinnati, Ohio. He comes from a remarkable family. His great-great-grandfather was a slave freed after the American Civil War. His grandfather, Harrison Wilson, Jr., was president of Norfolk State University, in Norfolk, Virginia. His father, Harrison Wilson III, played football and baseball at Dartmouth College, and became a lawyer. But Harrison Wilson III was a good enough wide receiver in football to almost make the San Diego Chargers team after graduating from law school. He was nicknamed "The Professor."

Russell Wilson's mother, Tammy T. Wilson, is a nurse and legal expert on nursing issues. She is a woman of deep faith and she has great knowledge of the Bible. *Seattle Times* reporter Danny O'Neil wrote that Tammy quotes scripture from memory, including a verse from Samuel: "The Lord does not look at the things people look at. People look at the outward appearance, but the Lord looks at the heart." She taught her children to be themselves and, "Don't be defined by what other people say."

By all accounts, the Wilsons were strict but loving parents. Family trips usually had a purpose and a lesson.

The family home was in the suburbs of Richmond, Virginia. When Russell was about five or six, he began to play catch with his father and older brother by five-and-a-half years, Harrison IV. Since his brother Harry wanted to be a receiver, Russell became the quarterback. They played both football and baseball.

The two boys were close, but rivals as well. Russell told ESPN reporter Chris Preston, "Whenever we'd compete against each other, it was pretty intense. It was like we didn't know each other."

Russell's younger sister, by nine years, Anna may be the best athlete in the family. She is among the country's most accomplished young female basketball players in her age group.

All three children went to Collegiate School, a private, expensive school in Richmond. Many children attended school there from kindergarten right through high school, as the Wilson children did.

Wilson was a good student, but not a model child. He confesses to being a bully when he was in grade school. He told ESPN reporter Terry Blount that "I was so competitive that I thought I owned the playground and thought I owned the classroom . . . I thought I was bigger than who I really was." He didn't think he would get in trouble for anything and he thought being mean would help him be liked by cool kids.

He told *Seahawks.com* writer Clare Farnsworth, "I used to get mad all the time. But for me, I've been graced with a great family, with people that really have encouraged me rather than discouraged me." It is possible that being one of the few African-Americans at the school made him feel out of place. That could make him angry, which in turn leads to bullying. A few trips to the principal's home with his father and a few warnings by caring teachers started to make him more mature.

He became more serious as a teenager. When he was about 14, he had a vivid dream about Jesus Christ. It changed him and made his religious faith much more important. He told Terry Blount, "I used to go to church to see cute girls. Now I go to work on my heart."

There was never any doubt about his extraordinary ability to run fast and throw hard. For a time, he was the ball boy for his brother's high school football team. At one game when he was in fifth grade, the referee yelled over to the sidelines for a new football. Instead of running it out, Russell threw a perfect spiral all the way across the field. The Collegiate football coach, Charlie McFall, took notice. He decided to keep his eyes on Wilson.

Wilson had a growth spurt early and that fueled his natural ability. He soon became a dominant player on both the Collegiate baseball and football teams. He led the football team to three straight state championships and was twice named the *Richmond Times-Dispatch* "Player of the Year." His coach, Charlie McFall, who had first noticed him when Russell was a ball boy, told Danny O'Neil of the *Seattle Times*, "I've never really seen or been around such a natural leader."

The Baltimore Orioles drafted Wilson in 2007 and offered him a million dollars to play baseball for them. But he had promised his father and himself that he would go to college. The University of Virginia decided to recruit a taller player to become their quarterback. So Russell Wilson enrolled at North Carolina State University in Raleigh, North Carolina, in the fall of 2007. He became a leader of the Wolfpack.

Wilson smacks a hit to help North Carolina State beat the University of Georgia in June 2008.

The Turning Point: Choosing Football

When Russell enrolled at North Carolina State, he told Chris Preston of ESPN, "I knew my whole life I wanted to play two sports in college . . . But being successful for me means being a leader in your community."

Leaders come in all shapes and sizes, but they have a few things in common. They have confidence in themselves and that inspires others to have confidence in them and follow their leadership. They are motivated to excel. And they have poise, the ability to be calm when things are getting crazy. Wilson was a leader by the time he got to North Carolina State, but he kept adding to his leadership skills after he got there. Leadership often means having a plan and a back-up plan. Russell usually has both for his life and on the field.

The plan was to not play football that first fall, but instead be "redshirted" so he could play four years after that. He did start on the baseball team his first spring, playing second and third base. North Carolina State baseball coach Elliott Avent told Preston, "He was a starter in the infield after only five weeks . . . He's a tremendous athlete, and his instincts are so good."

Wilson's work ethic also helped him as a player and leader. He often hit the weight room at five in the morning before class. He got faster and stronger. He usually lifted weights four days a week and worked on his agility and quickness three days a week. He never took a day off.

> *He usually lifted weights four days a week and worked on his agility and quickness three days a week. He never took a day off.*

In the summer of 2008, Wilson competed with many others to be the starting quarterback for the North Carolina State Wolfpack. Naturally, he won the job. Coach Avent told Preston, "Russell handles both sports as well as anybody I've ever seen . . . He's such a positive guy — he always has a smile on his face." When students say they don't have time to do things, Avent tells them the Russell Wilson story.

During his first year, Wilson's uncle Ben drove Russell's father to games at Carter Finley Stadium in Raleigh, North Carolina. Uncle Ben had to describe the action to his brother, because Harrison III's sight was failing. In one game against Wake Forest, Ben described Russell's scrambling out of the pocket, running left and then right to avoid tacklers. He told of a long and beautiful touchdown pass. But Russell's father could hear the roars of the crowd. There was nothing wrong with his hearing.

In June 2010, Russell was drafted by the Colorado Rockies to play second base. He drove to Richmond to tell his ailing father the good news. His father was in a coma, but Russell sensed that he could hear him. His father died the next day.

Twelve hundred people came to his father's funeral. *New York Times* writer Pete Thamel wrote that Harry told the story at the service about the day Harry intercepted a pass and was looking back to see if any defenders were chasing him. Instead, he saw his father in his business suit running down the sideline near him. "He's always been by our side. To me, that depicted who he was."

Wilson played in the minor leagues for the Rockies in the summer of 2010, and was ready to report for spring training with them in 2011. North Carolina football coach Tom O'Brien felt that Russell had to choose between football and baseball. Wilson wanted to continue to play both sports, as he had promised his father and himself that he would do. O'Brien told Wilson if he didn't give up baseball, he would no longer be the starting quarterback. Russell was hurt and angry. He had passed for more than eight thousand yards and seventy-six touchdowns and led North Carolina State to bowl games. He had improved each year. And he had graduated from North Carolina State in three years, majoring in communications and broadcasting, with a 4.0 grade-point average.

So, Wilson faced some big decisions. He chose to keep playing baseball for the Rockies in the minors and transfer to the University of Wisconsin for his senior year. Football coach Bret Bielema had heard about Wilson and recruited him.

Russell and his best friend Scott Pickett drove a U-Haul from Raleigh to Madison, Wisconsin. Wilson reported to the football stadium, picked up his football playbook, and started studying it moments after he arrived. He was not someone who liked to waste time. Coach Bielema was impressed.

Wilson's legend at the University of Wisconsin began the day he was given a challenge by one of the wide receivers in practice. He bet Wilson that he could not hit the crossbar with a football passed from 40 yards away. Wilson smiled and threw a rocket that clanged off the metal bar, echoing through Camp Randall Stadium. He was elected team captain soon after that. He led the Wisconsin Badgers to an 11-to-3 record and to the Rose Bowl. Wilson was great at both passing and running. He made fans cheer.

> *"I want to put all my focus in football and see where it takes me. I know that I have the talent, aptitude, and leadership to succeed on the next level," said Russell Wilson.*

January 2012 brought two life-changing events for Wilson. He married Ashton Meem on January 14, 2012, at the Country Club of Virginia, in Richmond. They had met in high school and dated long distance when she went to the University of Georgia.

Russell made the decision to choose football over baseball. He told the world, and Thamel, "I want to put all my focus in football and see where it takes me. I know that I have the talent, aptitude, and leadership to succeed on the next level." He told the Rockies he would not be returning for a third season in the minor leagues. Instead, he would skip a honeymoon and would train to sharpen his skills for the NFL draft. He would show pro coaches that his height didn't matter; that they should believe in his success and leadership. One team did believe, and it led them to the Super Bowl.

Many scouts were watching Wilson when he practiced for the
Senior Bowl in Mobile, Alabama, in January 2012.

Wilson shows that the key to throwing a perfect spiral pass is the wrist twist that leaves the pinky facing upwards and the palm facing outwards.

Flying High as a Seahawk

*T*he Seattle Seahawks drafted Russell Wilson in April 2012. He was the 75th pick and the sixth quarterback drafted. Andrew Luck was drafted first and Robert Griffin III was drafted second. Wilson wasn't drafted earlier because at five feet eleven inches (180.3 centimeters) he was about three inches shorter than what experts thought a professional quarterback should be. The success of Drew Brees at six feet tall (182.9 centimeters) had been a fluke, many thought. For a player to be able to see over tall onrushing linemen was simply more difficult for anyone under six feet tall.

Rookies don't usually start in the NFL. But Wilson did so well in the preseason practice that he won the job. Coach Pete Carroll told *Sports Illustrated Kids* reporter Christina Tapper, "When we gave Russell the job, I thought, 'Well, buckle up. It's gonna' be a Disney ride.'"

The ride became fun and exciting when the Seahawks played the feared New England Patriots on October 14, 2012, at Century Link Field in Seattle. The Seahawks were losing 23 to 17 late in the fourth quarter. They had the ball at their forty-three-yard line. Wilson took the ball and faked a handoff. He looked down the field, searching for an open receiver. Sidney Rice made a double move on the Patriot defense and he was open. Wilson saw him and threw a long pass. Rice told *Sports Illustrated Kids* reporters later, "It was a heck of a throw. When I came out of my break, the whole time I was looking at the ball in the air and it was so pretty . . . I was like 'You've got to catch up to it.'" He caught it and the Seahawks won 24 to 23. Seattle safety Earl Thomas told reporters, "If guys didn't believe in [Wilson before], I guarantee they believe in him now."

> *Everyone Wilson knew wanted tickets to the game and he joked that he would have to ask Redskins quarterback Robert Griffin III for some tickets.*

If that game didn't make believers out of his teammates, the game against the Chicago Bears on December 2, 2012, did. Wilson threw two late touchdown passes to bring the game to overtime. He then threw a long touchdown to Rice to win the game, 23 to 17. Defensive back Richard Sherman told Larry Stone of the *Seattle Times*, "He played outside of his mind . . . He ran it when he had to, he threw great passes when he had to and drove the ball down the field when he had to for a game-winner."

Wilson led the Seahawks to the playoffs. On January 6, 2013, at FedEx Field in Landover, Maryland, they battled the Washington Redskins. It was a homecoming for Wilson. Everyone he knew wanted tickets to the game and he joked that he would have to ask Redskins quarterback Robert Griffin III for some tickets.

Wilson not only worked his magic passing and running, he threw a key block in the fourth quarter that allowed Marshawn Lynch to score the go-ahead touchdown. It was a Seahawks win at 24 to 14.

But the next week the Seahawks came back down to earth. Russell Wilson led his team on four touchdown drives in the second half against the Atlanta Falcons. But that just came up short, and the Falcons won 30 to 28.

In the tunnel leading to the locker room after the game, Wilson was already thinking about next year. It would be a year to remember.

A blizzard of confetti and fan appreciation surrounds the Super-Bowl-winning Seahawks in downtown Seattle on February 5, 2014.

State dinners at the White House are formal and important affairs, and here Wilson and his date Ciara Harris help honor the Japanese Prime Minister in April 2015.

Turning on the Magic

Wilson reacted to the playoff loss by asking himself how he could get better. He told Terry Blount of the *Seattle Times* "I'm extremely critical of myself, but in a positive way. I try to understand . . . how I can do it better."

By "it" Wilson seems to mean everything. He has always thought that he needed to do things for his community. Soon after arriving in Seattle, he called the Seattle Children's Hospital and asked what he could do to help. Hospital officials must have expected a photo opportunity once or twice in a playroom with sick children. Athletes often do that for good publicity. But the Wilsons were different. They kept coming every Tuesday. And they wanted to visit the children and their parents in the hospital rooms, to spend time with them away from cameras.

Chris and Mindie Sayers's daughter Abi was born prematurely. She had heart and lung problems and she fought for her tiny, young life in the hospital. Wilson visited the Sayers. Chris told ESPN's Kevin Van Valkenburg, "He kept coming back to visit us. He never wanted to talk about himself, he just wanted to give us a hug and ask how Abi was doing . . . I believe in my heart that he's genuine."

Hospital executive Eve Koss told Van Valkenburg, "He's an avid Christian, and he wants to walk the talk. I think his dad is in his heart every time he goes room to room. I think it's something that would have made his dad very proud."

Wilson started the "Why Not You Foundation" to raise money and awareness for a number of causes. The first cause was to fight domestic violence. An initiative called "Pass the Peace" tries to make more people aware of the issue.

But his community and charity work would have to divide time with his football work. In the middle of the 2013 season, Wilson's game had slumped and he was not making plays the way he wanted to. He told Terry Blount of the

Wilson's speed and quickness left many New England Patriot defenders out of the picture in Super Bowl XLIX on February 1, 2015.

Wilson hands off to Robert Turbin during Super Bowl XLIX as the Seahawk offense tries to grind down the Patriot defense with more runs than passes early in the game.

Seattle Times, "I think my dad would tell me, 'Just be poised, Russ.' He told me to always be the calm in the storm. He told me to keep believing in yourself."

Sure enough, Wilson rallied himself and his team and won a crucial game against the St. Louis Rams, on December 29, 2013. That began the run of wins that ended in his brilliant Super Bowl performance.

Wilson continues to lead and inspire. On September 21, 2014, the Seahawks and Broncos met in a Super Bowl rematch. Unlike their Super Bowl game of a few months earlier, it was a classic and close game. In overtime, Wilson couldn't be stopped. He scrambled outside the pocket and completed pass after pass when he wasn't running for first downs. He drove the team 80 yards for the winning touchdown. The Seahawks won 26 to 20.

He set a record on Monday Night Football (MNF) on October 6, 2014. He ran for 122 yards, the most ever by a quarterback on MNF. He told *Seattle Times* reporter Jerry Brewer, "I don't think running for me is ever part of the game plan . . . It just kind of happens." In that game against the Redskins at FedEx Field, the Seahawks were trying to hold on to a 24 to 17 lead late in the game. Wilson took a snap, spun to his left to avoid the defensive linemen, ran all the way to near the left sideline and then suddenly lofted a soft pass to running back Marshawn Lynch. The defenders thought he was running out of bounds or would throw it away. But Wilson never stopped looking downfield, the mark of a great quarterback. Brewer wrote, "Wilson can turn on the magic. And he just shrugs. No big deal."

> *"I don't think running for me is ever part of the game plan . . . It just kind of happens,"* says Russell Wilson.

As he did in the middle of the 2013 season, Wilson slumped in the middle of the 2014 season. He went four straight games with below average (for him) performances. But when his team needed him most, against the division-leading Arizona Cardinals on November 23, 2014, Wilson came up big again. He was being battered by the Cardinals' ferocious defense, one of the league's best. In the third quarter, Arizona linebacker Alex Okafor broke loose from his blocker and chased Wilson back almost 20 yards. But Wilson somehow found a way to pass to Marshawn Lynch for a 23-yard gain. Coach Carroll told *Seattle Times* Bob Candotta that the play "showed that magic." The Seahawks won that crucial game, 19 to 3.

But the Cardinals were looking for revenge in a game to decide first place in the division, on December 21, 2014. On one fourth-quarter play, Wilson took the hike and faked a handoff. He started running to his left. The Cardinal defenders were waiting for him. They had already seen this play many times. Wilson stopped and looked to his right. The Arizona linebacker watched his eyes, but Wilson fooled him and ran around him. One of Arizona's best tacklers, Antonio Cromartie, closed in. But again Wilson stopped, faked right, and moved left, leaving Cromartie to grasp for air. Wilson scored a touchdown and looked down humbly. He didn't celebrate. No big deal. The Cardinals' spirit seemed broken. Seahawks won easily with late scores, 35 to 6.

Wilson scored a touchdown and looked down humbly. He didn't celebrate. No big deal.

Wilson and the Seahawks are now battle-tested. Wilson's running and passing magic casts a spell and breaks opponents' spirits. But it is also Russell Wilson's gifts of leadership and faith that have united his teammates and his city. And when a small sick girl in the Seattle Children's Hospital hears his voice, she knows that something good is about to happen.

1988	Russell Carrington Wilson is born on November 29, in Cincinnati, Ohio; his father is Harrison Wilson III and his mother is Tammy Wilson.
2005	Wilson is named All-State football player at Collegiate School and is named Richmond *Times-Dispatch* Player of the Year.
2006	Wilson is elected senior class president at Collegiate School. Again, he is named All-State and *Times-Dispatch* Player of the Year in football.
2007	In June, Russell is drafted by the Baltimore Orioles to play baseball; instead, he enters North Carolina State University, in Raleigh, North Carolina.
2008	Wilson is named first-team All-Atlantic-Conference quarterback.
2009	On September 19, Wilson sets the NCAA record for most consecutive pass attempts (325) without an interception.
2010	Wilson graduates from North Carolina State in May with a degree in communications. On June 8, he is drafted by the Colorado Rockies and plays minor league baseball in the summer.
2011	In January, Wilson notifies North Carolina State football coach Tom O'Brien that he will go to spring training with the Colorado Rockies and miss spring football practice. On April 29, Wilson is released from his scholarship. On June 27, Wilson announces that he will spend his senior year at the University of Wisconsin. In December, Wilson is named to All-Big Ten first team, and third team All-American.
2012	On January 2, Wilson and the Wisconsin Badgers play in the Rose Bowl, and lose forty-five to thirty-eight. He is drafted by the Seattle Seahawks on April 27. On September 9, he plays in his first regular season game as a starter.
2013	Wilson plays in his first Pro Bowl and throws three touchdown passes.
2014	Wilson and the Seahawks win the Super Bowl on February 2. He takes part in the Seattle victory parade on February 5.
2015	Wilson led the Seahawks to an overtime win against the Green Bay Packers on January 18, to bring the team back to the Super Bowl. In one of the most famous plays in Super Bowl history, New England Patriot Malcolm Butler intercepted Wilson's last pass of the game to give the Patriots a 28-24 victory on February 1. Wilson takes on a new challenge by hosting the 2015 Kids' Choice Sports Awards.

STATISTICS

Season	TEAM	GP	CMP	ATT	YDS	AVG	TD	LNG	INT	FUM
2012	SEA	16	252	393	3,118	7.93	26	67	10	3
2013	SEA	16	257	407	3,357	8.25	26	80	9	8
2014	SEA	16	285	452	3,475	7.69	20	80	7	6
Career		48	794	1,252	9,950	7.95	72	80	26	17

GP- Games Played, CMP- Yds Completed, ATT- Passes Attempted, YDS-
Passing Yds, AVG- Yards per pass attempt, TD- Passing Touchdowns, LNG-
Longest Pass play, INT-Interceptions, FUM- Fumbles

AWARDS

2005 All-State player in football. *Richmond Times-Dispatch* Player of the Year.

2006 All-State player in football. Senior class president, Collegiate School.

2008 First-team All-Atlantic Conference as quarterback.

2009 Sets NCAA record for most consecutive pass attempts (325) without an interception.

2011 All-Big Ten first team, All-American third team, Big Ten Quarterback of the Year.

2012 NFC Offensive Player of the Week, week 13; NFL Offensive Player of the Month, December; Pepsi NFL Rookie of the Year; tied for most touchdown passes by a rookie (26), tied with Peyton Manning. Highest rookie quarterback rating (100.0).

2013 Most regular season wins by a quarterback in his first two seasons (24). Voted to Pro Bowl.

2014 Super Bowl XLVIII Champion. Most wins by a quarterback in first three seasons in the Super Bowl era (35).

2015 The Salvation Army honored Wilson with its Arthur S. Langlie Award for Visionary Leadership.

FURTHER READING

Books

Blount, Terry. "Russell Wilson: Never Doubted 'Mates." *ESPN.com*, October 27, 2014.http://espn.go.com/nfl/story/_/id/11769374/russell-wilson-says-seattle-seahawks-locker-room-closest-ever-been

Chadiha, Jeffri. "Russell Wilson on Path to Greatness." *ESPN.com*, April 4, 2014. http://espn.go.com/nfl/story/_/id/10725050/russell-wilson-career-tom-brady-path

Durrett, Richard. "Russell Wilson Wants to be Best Ever." *ESPN.com*, April 3, 2014. http://espn.go.com/dallas/nfl/story/_/id/10719020/russell-wilson-seattle-seahawks-wants-best-qb-nfl-history

Works Consulted

Blount, Terry. "Russell Wilson Explains Pass the Peace." *ESPN.com*, October 3, 2014.http://espn.go.com/blog/seattle-seahawks/post/_/id-9022/wilson-explains-pass-the-peace

Brewer, Jerry. "Russell Wilson Saves Seahawks From Themselves." *The Seattle Times*, October 7, 2014. http://seattletimes.com/html/jerrybrewer/2024716129_brewerseahawks07xml.html

Condotta, Bob. "With Russell Wilson Trusting Himself and His Teammates, Seahawks Score a 19-3 Victory." *The Seattle Times*, November 23, 2014. http://seattletimes.com/html/seahawks/2025087504_seahawkssidebarcondotta24.xml.html

Farnsworth, Clare. "Russell Wilson Wants You to 'Pass the Peace.' " *Seahawks.com*, October 3, 2014. http://www.chatsports.com/seattle-seahawks/a/Russell-Wilson-wants-you-to-Pass-the-Peace-1-10503157

Keim, John. "Seahawks Praised at White House." *ESPN.com*, May 22, 2014. http://espn.go.com/nfl/story/_/id/10965509/super-bowl-champion-seattle-seahawks-visit-the-white-house-praised-president-barack-obama

O'Neil, Danny. "Russell Wilson Defied All Odds to Become the Talk of the NFL." *The Seattle Times*, December 22, 2012. http://seattletimes.com/html/seahawks/2019965454_wilson23.html

Preston, Chris. "Wolfpack's Wilson Living a Dream as Two-sport College Athlete." *ESPN.com*, July 31, 2008. http://sports.espn.go.com/ncaa/news/story?id=3512366

Rhoden, William C. "For Seattle's Celebration, Russell Wilson Is an Unofficial M.V.P." *The New York Times*, February 5, 2014. http://www.nytimes.com/2014/02/06/sports/football/for-seattles-celebration-russell-wilson-is-an-unofficial-mvp.html

Tapper, Christina. "NFL Preview 2013: Seattle Seahawks Quarterback Russell Wilson, Standing Tall." *Sports Illustrated Kids*, September 13, 2013. http://www.sikids.com/blogs/2013/09/13/nfl-preview-2013-seattle-seahawks-quarterback-russell-wilson-standing-tall

Thamel, Pete. "Russell Wilson Puts Wisconsin on Target for Title Run." *The New York Times*, August 26, 2011. http://www.nytimes.com/2011/08/28/sports/ncaafootball/new-quarterback-puts-wisconsin-on-target-for-the-title-run.html

Thamel, Pete. "Wisconsin Quarterback Opts for Football Career." *The New York Times*, January 11, 2012.http://www.nytimes.com/2012/01/12/sports/ncaafootball/russell-wilson-of-wisconsin-picks-football-over-baseball.html

Van Valkenburg, Kevin. "The Adoration of Russell Wilson." *ESPN.com*, January 31, 2014.http://espn.go.com/nfl/playoffs/2013/story/_/id/10371865/super-bowl-xlviii-why-seattle-fans-adore-russell-wilson

On the Internet

Seattle Seahawks
http://www.seahawks.com.

"Seattle Seahawks Are Super Bowl Champs!" *Sports Illustrated Kids*, February 3, 2014. http://www.sikids.com/blogs/2014/02/03/seattle-seahawks-are-super-bowl-champs

PHOTO CREDITS: p. 4—Mark Cornelison/MCT/Newscom; p. 8, 12—Ethan Hyman/MCT/Newscom; p. 17—Melinda Dove | Dreamstime.com; p. 18—George Holland/Cal Sport Media/Newscom; p. 21—Angie Westre | Dreamstime.com; p. 22—Olivier Douliery / Pool via CNP; p. 24—Ronald Martinez/Getty Images; p. 25—Focus on Sport/Getty Images.

INDEX